Longman Structural Reader
Stage 2

Scotland

David Hill

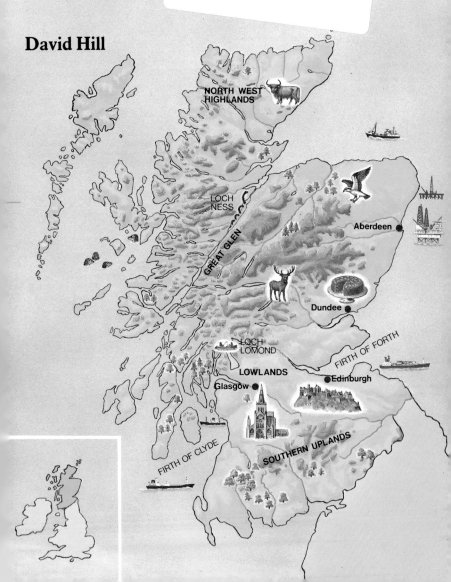

NORTH WEST
HIGHLANDS

35 Skye

32 LOCH
NESS

34 CULLODEN MOOR

31 CAIRNGORMS

22 Aberdeen

26 Balmoral Castle

GRAMPIAN HIGHLANDS

GREAT GLEN

BEN NEVIS

36 GLEN COE

Dundee

20 FIRTH OF TAY

19 Perth

21 St Andrews

37 LOCH
LOMOND

18 Stirling

18 FIRTH OF FORTH

LOWLANDS

9 Tantallon Castle

40 Glasgow

10 Edinburgh

42 New Lanark

5 Berwick
upon Tweed

44 Ayr

SOUTHERN UPLANDS

6 THE BORDERS

44 FIRTH OF CLYDE

46 Dumfries

*The numbers on the map
are the numbers of the pages
in the book.*

The geography of Scotland

Scotland is the north part of Great Britain. This part is full of mountains and lakes. The highest mountain is Ben Nevis (1,343 m) and there are several mountains over 1,000 m high. There are a lot of lakes. The Scottish word *loch* names an arm of the sea or an inland lake. The biggest inland lake is Loch Lomond. It is 36 kilometres long.

The sea nearly cuts the mountains into three parts. The Firth of Clyde and the Firth of Forth come between the Southern Uplands and the Grampian Highlands. The Great Glen and Loch Ness come between the Grampian Highlands and the North Western Highlands.

Five million people live in Scotland. A lot of people live in the Lowlands, between the Clyde and the Forth. Glasgow, the largest city, is on the Clyde. Edinburgh, the capital, is on the Forth. There are two other large cities: Dundee and Aberdeen.

The history of Scotland

500 BC – 0 AD	The Celts	
0 AD – 500	The Romans	In 81 the Romans came to Scotland. In 141 the Romans built a wall from the Forth to the Clyde. About 380 the Romans left Scotland.
500 – 1000	Four kings	For 500 years Scotland was four countries with four kings. In 563 St Columba brought Christianity from Ireland.

		In 1034 Duncan was king of all Scotland.
1000 – 1500	The English	In 1296 the English king came to Scotland with an army. In 1314 the Scots and the English met at Bannockburn near Stirling. The Scots killed a lot of English soldiers, so the English king went back to England.
1500 – the present	Great Britain	In 1603 King James VI became King of England as well. The King's new title was "King of Great Britain". In 1707 both the Scottish parliament and the English parliament became one parliament in London.

The flags of Scotland, England and the United Kingdom

The Scottish flag is a white cross on a blue background. The cross is the cross of Saint Andrew. Saint Andrew was a friend of Jesus and the brother of Saint Peter.

The English flag is a red cross on a white background. The cross is the cross of Saint George.

This is the Union Jack. It is the flag of the United Kingdom of Great Britain and Northern Ireland. You can see the white cross of Saint Andrew and the red cross of Saint George.

A visit to Scotland

Some people go to Scotland in a plane. Some people go to Scotland in a ship. But a lot of people go to Scotland in a train or a car from England.

There are trains and buses to Glasgow and Edinburgh from London every day but let's go in a car. We shall go up the east side of Scotland and come down the west side.

We enter Scotland near Berwick on Tweed. (See 5 on the map at the front of the book.)

The Borders

This part of Scotland is very beautiful. The River Tweed begins in the Southern Uplands and goes east through the hills into the North Sea. In the river there are many salmon. Salmon are fish. They have pink meat and they cost a lot of money in the shops.

A long time ago the Scots built many large churches beside the river. These churches were called Abbeys. In the picture you can see the ruins of Melrose Abbey. The Scots built Melrose Abbey in 1136 but the English destroyed it in 1544.

In the days of the Abbeys, the hills and the farms of the Borders were full of sheep and they still are.

Sir Walter Scott (1771–1832)

Sir Walter Scott loved the Borders. In his early years, the boy Walter lived with his grandfather near Kelso. He walked over the hills and listened to the stories of the farmers.

He went to school and university in Edinburgh. After that, he worked at Selkirk for a few years. He talked to the old men and women and listened to their stories. He used these stories in his books.

We can visit Abbotsford beside the River Tweed. Scott built this house in 1817. We can see his desk, his chair, his books and his pictures. He died here in 1832.

Lucia di Lammermoor

Sir Walter wrote a sad story about Lucy Ashton. She lived in a big house in the Lammermuir Hills.

Lucy loved a poor man called Edgar. She wanted to marry Edgar but her brother did not agree.

Edgar went to Italy for a year. He wrote letters to Lucy, but her brother did not give the letters to Lucy. He told Lucy, "Edgar does not write letters to you. He does not love you. You must marry my rich friend." Lucy said yes and married the rich man.

On the same day Edgar came back. Lucy was very sad and became very ill. She killed her husband. Then she died soon after. Edgar was very sad. He put a knife into his body and he also died.

Perhaps you know the opera about Lucy by Donnizetti. It is called *Lucia di Lammermoor*. This is a picture from the opera. It shows Lucia. The blood on her dress is her husband's blood.

Tantallon Castle and the Bass Rock

Now we leave the Borders and go up into the Lammermuir Hills. These hills are not very high, but from the top we can see the Firth of Forth and Edinburgh.

There are a lot of castles in this part of Scotland. One of the largest is Tantallon Castle. You can see it in the picture. The Douglas family built it six hundred years ago, but the English destroyed it in 1651.

Near Tantallon Castle you can see the Bass Rock. It is a small island, 100 metres high. A long time ago there was a prison on the rock. Now there is a lighthouse, and many thousands of birds live on the island.

The City of Edinburgh

Now we go west towards Edinburgh. First we can see Arthur's Seat, a hill in the middle of the city. Visitors to Edinburgh like to go up this hill. From the top (250 m) they can see all the city and the sea and the hills.

Arthur's Seat is the highest hill in Edinburgh, but the most important hill is the Rock. It is 1.6 km long. At the top end (137 m) the Scots built the Castle (in the picture above) and at the bottom end they built the Palace of Holyrood House.

We must visit the Castle and walk down the long street to Holyrood House. This street is called the Royal Mile. The stone houses are three or four hundred years old.

Mary Queen of Scots

Mary Queen of Scots lived in Holyrood House for six years from 1561 to 1567. The story of her life is a very sad one.

Mary was born on 8 December 1542. Her father, King James V of Scotland, died one week later, so Mary became queen when she was one week old.

In 1548 she went to France and in 1558 she married the first son of the King of France. She was very happy in France, but after two years her husband died. The next year she came back to Scotland and lived in Holyrood House.

In those days there were Catholic Christians and Protestant Christians in Europe. Mary was a Catholic, but very many Scots were Protestant and did not like Mary. Their leader was John Knox and you can see his house near Holyrood House.

Mary at Holyrood House

In 1565 Mary married Lord Darnley and in 1566 she had a baby. The baby's name was James. Darnley was tall and handsome, but he was a Protestant, and soon Mary and Darnley were enemies.

Darnley and his friends killed David Rizzio, Mary's Italian secretary. A year later Darnley died. Some men started a fire in his house. Darnley ran outside and the men killed him in the garden. Were these men friends of Mary? We do not know. Mary married again and her third husband was Lord Bothwell.

Bothwell tried to help Mary, but her enemies were too strong. They put Mary in prison and took away her son James. Bothwell left Scotland and went to Norway.

Lord Darnley ▲
The murder of Rizzio ▼

Mary in England

Mary was in prison on an island in Loch Leven. Here she met
Willie Douglas. He was only a young boy but he liked Mary
and wanted to help her. One day he took the keys of the castle
and led Mary out of her room and out of the castle. Then he
put Mary in a boat and took her to her friends. Mary's friends
had an army, but her enemies were too strong and she had to
leave Scotland.

Mary could not go to France because there was no boat. She
went to England and asked Queen Elizabeth for help.
Elizabeth was her cousin, but she did not help Mary.
Elizabeth was Protestant and she did not want a Catholic
queen in Scotland. So she kept Mary in prison.

Mary's Catholic friends tried to help her. The Pope and the
Catholic King of Spain agreed to send an army against
Elizabeth. The Protestant people of England were afraid. In
1586 they said, "Mary must die". Elizabeth had to agree.

In 1603 Elizabeth died. She had no children, so Mary's son
James became King of Scotland and England.

The new town

Two hundred years later, in the 1760s, the people of Edinburgh started to build the new town.

The new town has three long straight streets: Queen Street, George Street and Princes Street. At the west end of George Street there is Charlotte Square, and at the east end there is St Andrew Square.

The most famous street in Edinburgh is Princes Street. On one side of the street there are shops and on the other side there are beautiful gardens. Many visitors go to the gardens and sit and listen to music.

The big picture shows Princes Street and the castle. The Scott Memorial, a tall building with a statue inside it of Sir Walter Scott, is at the end of Princes Street.

Great men of Edinburgh

David Hume (1711–1776) wrote important books on history and philosophy and was a teacher at the university.

Adam Smith (1723–1790) wrote a very important book on economics and taught at the university.

Henry Raeburn (1756–1823) painted pictures of rich men and women.

Robert Adam (1728–1792) built many houses in the new town.

Robert Louis Stevenson (1850–1894) wrote story books. *Treasure Island* and *Kidnapped* are both about boys.

Bad men of Edinburgh

In 1829 there were many medical students in Edinburgh. They wanted to learn about the human body, and so they had to cut up dead bodies. But their teachers could not get dead bodies easily. Only one teacher, Dr Knox, could easily get bodies. He bought them from two men, Burke and Hare. He paid £10 for each body in winter and £8 in summer.

How did Burke and Hare get the bodies? They killed people, and sold the bodies to Dr Knox. One day the students saw the body of a friend. They asked questions and soon Burke and Hare were in prison. The picture shows the death of Burke.

The Festival

Every summer thousands of people visit Edinburgh for the Festival. They can listen to music and watch plays and look at pictures. Every day for three weeks, visitors and Edinburgh people can see and do many different things in the mornings, the afternoons and the evenings.

One evening there is a firework display. On that evening there are no cars or buses in Princes Street. Princes Street and the gardens are full of people. They listen to music and watch the fireworks in the sky above the castle.

On other evenings there is the Tattoo. This is in the castle. Soldiers from different countries march inside the castle. There is music from Scottish pipers and other bands. Soldiers, seamen and airmen show their different skills. At the end of the evening, one piper plays his pipes on the walls of the castle.

The Forth bridges

We must leave Edinburgh. 8 miles (12 km) west of the city we come to Queensferry. There was once a ferry here across the Firth of Forth to Fife, but now there are two large bridges.

One bridge carries the railway. The first train crossed the bridge in 1878. The part of the bridge over the water is 2,526 metres long. The colour of the bridge is red and it takes three years to paint it.

The other bridge carries the road. The first cars and buses went across in 1972. The part of the bridge over the sea is 1,876 metres long.

We can look at the great bridges but we do not want to go across the water. We stay on the south and go to Stirling.

The battle of Bannockburn

In the old days, the first bridge across the River Forth was at Stirling. Here there is a great rock with a castle on it. In 1314 the English held the castle and the Scots and their king, Robert Bruce, attacked it.

The English sent an army to the castle. Bruce and his

soldiers attacked the English army at Bannockburn, near Stirling. The Scots killed many English soldiers, and Bruce killed an English general. The English King Edward II ran away to England. After that the English came to Scotland many times but they could never stay there.

The Fair Maid of Perth

Perth is famous now for its whisky. But in the 14th century it was famous for a battle. Sir Walter Scott wrote about this battle in his story of *The Fair Maid of Perth*, and Bizet used the story for his opera.

The Fair Maid (= beautiful girl) was Catharine Glover, daughter of Simon Glover, a merchant. Three men loved her: the son of a Highland chief, a soldier and maker of swords, and a son of the king. In the story, the highlander dies in the river, the king's son dies in battle at Perth and the soldier marries Catharine.

Macbeth

In Shakespeare's play *Macbeth*, Birnam Wood comes to Dunsinane. Dunsinane is outside Perth and Birnam Wood is 20 miles (32 km) north.

In the play Lady Macbeth tells Macbeth to kill King Duncan. Macbeth becomes king and his wife becomes queen. But they are not happy. They are always afraid. They kill their enemies but Malcolm, Duncan's son, gets to England.

Malcolm brings an army to Scotland. He wants to hide the size of his army. So his soldiers have to carry branches of trees from Birnam Wood. Macbeth cannot see the soldiers. There is a battle and Macbeth dies.

In real history, Macbeth was a good king and he did not kill Duncan.

The Tay bridges

In the picture on page 21 you can see the old railway bridge and the new road bridge across the Firth of Tay. But the railway bridge is the second bridge. The first bridge fell down.

The first train crossed the first bridge in 1878. The last train went onto the bridge on the evening of December 28th 1879. It never reached the other side. There was a very strong wind that night. The bridge broke and the train fell into the sea. 48 people died.

Golf

Not far from the Tay bridges we come to St Andrews. This small town has had a university since 1410 but now it is also famous for golf.

There are several golf courses at St Andrews. The Royal and Ancient Golf Club is one of them and it is very important for players of golf.

There are other important golf courses in Scotland. Players come from other countries to play at Gleneagles (near Perth), Muirfield (near Edinburgh), Prestwick and Turnberry (near Ayr). The big courses are expensive but the small courses are cheap, so many Scottish people play golf in summer and winter.

Aberdeen

Now we will travel north from the Tay Bridge and after 65 miles (104 km) we will come to Aberdeen, the granite city. Granite is a hard grey stone and Aberdeen people build their houses with granite. The most famous street is Union Street. This runs from the harbour in a straight line for one mile (1.6 km).

Aberdeen has a big harbour. Ships come to Aberdeen from northern Europe. Aberdeen was once famous for fish but now it is famous for oil. Oil companies have their offices here, and oil company men have their homes here.

North Sea oil and gas

The North Sea lies between Scotland and Denmark. The water is not very deep. But in winter the weather can be very bad. Strong winds blow, with rain and snow, and the waves can be 10 metres high.

The North Sea was famous only for its fish. Now it is famous for oil and gas. The British found the first oil under their part of the North Sea in 1969. They first took oil from an oil well in 1975. In 1980, they got all their oil from the North Sea oil wells and did not have to buy any from other countries. In 1982 they were the fifth largest oil country after the USSR, the USA, Saudi Arabia and Mexico.

In 1965 the British found gas under the North Sea, and in 1970 they brought the first gas from the North Sea to the land in a pipe. Most North Sea gas comes to a refinery near Aberdeen. From there it goes in pipes all over the country. Before 1970 all British gas came from coal. Now it nearly all comes from the North Sea and it will come from there for ten or fifteen years.

KEY
Oil field
Gas field
Oil well
Gas well
Oil & Gas well

Brent

Clair

Shetland Islands

Orkney Islands

Hebrides

Beatrice
MORAY FIRTH

Claymore   Piper

Scotland

Ettrick
Buchan   Forties

ABERDEEN

Gannet

DUNDEE

FIRTH OF FORTH

Clyde   Ekofisk
Auk

GLASGOW

FIRTH OF
CLYDE

Balmoral Castle

We will now leave Aberdeen and the North Sea and go up the River Dee. Soon we come to Balmoral Castle.

Queen Victoria and her husband Prince Albert liked to stay at Balmoral in the summer. They first came here in 1848. After the death of Prince Albert in 1861, Victoria came here with her family and painted many pictures of the hills and mountains.

Queen Elizabeth and her family go to Scotland every year in the summer. They spend two weeks in Holyrood House in Edinburgh and then go to Balmoral. The picture shows the Queen on holiday at Balmoral.

The kilt

In the picture the Queen is wearing a kilt. Both men and women wear kilts but men also wear a sporran. A sporran is a small bag.

In the 17th century the people of the highlands, the highlanders, did not wear trousers. They wore kilts. They made the kilts of tartan, a kind of cloth with coloured squares.

The highlanders also wore tartan cloth over their shoulders instead of a coat.

In the 19th century the tartan cloth became very popular. Everyone wanted to wear the kilt. On the next page you can see a highlander of the 18th century and two highlanders of today.

The Scottish clans

The highlanders speak English but some of them also speak Gaelic. Every highlander is a member of one of the big families, or clans, of Scotland, and all the people of one clan have the same name and wear the same tartan. On this page you can see the names of some of the famous clans.

Campbell	Macdonald
Fraser	Mackinnon
Munro	Macgregor
Cameron	Macfie
Stewart	Maclean
Royal Stuart	Mackenzie
Murray	Macleod

The bagpipes

The highlanders play music on the bagpipes. The piper blows air into a bag. He holds this bag under his arm and presses the air into the other pipes. In this way the music never stops.

The bagpipes make a very loud sound and you can hear the pipes a long way away. Some of the tunes are very famous and you can hear them at the Tattoo at the Edinburgh Festival.

Scottish country dancing

Everybody likes the tartan and the bagpipes. Everybody also likes to dance the Scottish dances. In the picture below there are four men and four women. They are dancing a reel. The men are wearing kilts and the women are wearing white dresses with a tartan sash.

Some reels are very difficult but others are very easy. Often the men stand in one line and the women in another.

The Highland Games

In the picture below you can see a man in a white vest and a kilt. He is holding a caber in his hands and he is going to toss (= throw) it. A caber is a long piece of wood and it comes from the trunk of a tree.

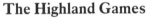

Another sport is to throw a very heavy weight. The usual weight for men at the Olympic Games is 16 pounds (7.2 kg), but the weight at the Highland Games is 24 pounds (10.8 kg).

You can go to these Games at Inverness, Crieff and other places.

The Cairngorms and Aviemore

We must walk from the River Dee to Aviemore because there is no road over the Cairngorm Mountains. Of course we can go by road, but it is a long way round.

The Cairngorms are over 1300 metres high. The mountains in Norway and Switzerland are higher than the Cairngorms but in winter the Cairngorms can be very cold and dangerous.

Many people go to the Cairngorms. In summer they walk and climb. In winter they ski. Most of these visitors stay at Aviemore. Here there are modern hotels, restaurants and lots of different kinds of entertainment.

Loch Ness and the monster

Many people today visit Loch Ness. Let's go there too. First we pass Culloden Moor (see page 34) and the town of Inverness. Then we enter the Great Glen (= Valley) between the Grampians and the Northern Highlands. Soon we come to Loch Ness.

Why do so many people come to Loch Ness? They want to see Nessie, the Loch Ness Monster. In 1934 a man called Robert Wilson took a photograph beside Loch Ness. Is it a monster in the photograph? No one knows, but the Loch is very deep and the water is very dark. Perhaps a monster lives at the bottom.

Bonnie Prince Charlie

In 1745 George II was King of Great Britain. But the highlanders did not like George. They liked Charles Edward Stuart. Charles was the grandson of James II but he was a Catholic, so he could not be king of Protestant England and Scotland.

Prince Charles went to Scotland from France and many highlanders joined him. From Holyrood House he led his army into England. But very few English people joined him, so he went back to Scotland. In 1746 his army fought against the English at Culloden Moor.

Culloden Moor

Prince Charles had 4,000 soldiers, a few horses and six guns. The men had no food on the day before the battle and no breakfast on the morning of the battle. Half of the soldiers tried to attack King George's army during the night but they lost their way and did not sleep at all. The weather was very cold. The soldiers were cold, tired and hungry.

The king's army had 6,400 soldiers, 2,400 horses and a lot of guns. They had good clothes and good guns. They slept before the battle and they had a good breakfast.

The highlanders ran forward across the moor. They had to run a mile and the English soldiers shot them down. 1,200 highlanders died and only 50 Englishmen. Prince Charles left the battle and tried to go to France.

Flora Macdonald

The English soldiers tried to find Bonnie Prince Charlie. They found many highland soldiers and killed them. But they did not find the Prince.

Charles went by boat to the islands of the Hebrides. Still the soldiers followed him. He went to the southern island and the soldiers followed him there. Here a lady helped him. Her name was Flora Macdonald. She gave him a woman's clothes. He put them on and then he was Flora's servant. The two "women" got into a boat and sailed to the Island of Skye.

Here they stayed quietly for a few weeks. Then a boat took Prince Charles to France. He lived in Italy until he died in 1786.

Glencoe

Our road now takes us south. We pass Fort William and Ben
Nevis, the highest mountain in Scotland. Then we come to
Glencoe, a steep and dark valley.

In 1692 the Campbells killed nearly 40 Macdonalds in
Glencoe. The Campbells hated the Macdonalds because in
1689 the Macdonalds took many of their sheep and cattle. Also
the Campbells were on the side of King William but the
Macdonalds were on King James's side.

The Campbells went to Glencoe and stayed with the
Macdonalds. For two weeks they were friends. Then early one
morning the Campbells set fire to the houses and started to kill
the Macdonalds. For this reason the Macdonalds still hate the
Campbells.

Loch Lomond

From Glencoe we cross Rannoch Moor and come down to
Loch Lomond. This is the largest lake in Britain. It is
thirty-six kilometers wide and eight kilometers long. Many
people visit the lake and spend the day there. It is near
Glasgow (page 40) and trains and buses can reach Loch
Lomond from Glasgow in one hour.

East of Loch Lomond are the lakes and hills called the
Trossachs. The Trossachs were the home of the Macgregor
clan. Sir Walter Scott's *Rob Roy* is a story about a brave leader
of the Macgregors.

The River Clyde

Five miles south of Loch Lomond we find the River Clyde. There are still some shipyards on this river but from 1800 to 1970 there were four big ones: Govan, Scotstoun, John Brown and Scott Lithgow.

The most famous ships from the Clyde are the *Queen Elizabeth*, the *Queen Mary* and the *Queen Elizabeth II (QE II)*.

Greenock is the largest town on the south bank of the river. It is famous for sugar.

Paisley is five miles south of the river. It is famous for cotton and the Singer sewing machines.

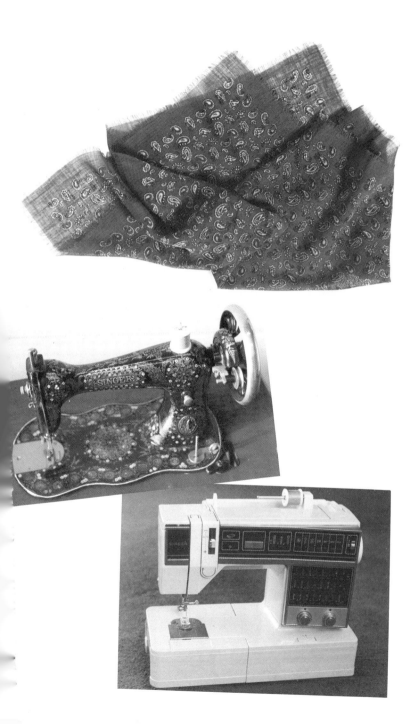

Glasgow

Glasgow is the largest city in Scotland and the third largest in the United Kingdom. 762,200 people live in Glasgow, and another 500,000 live in towns close to Glasgow.

Before 1750 Glasgow was a small town. It had a cathedral and a university but it was not a rich town.

After 1707 Scottish ships could go to the English colonies in America. Ships brought tobacco to Glasgow and took back Scottish goods. One of the famous tobacco men was George Buchanan, and we can walk in Buchanan Street today.

In 1776, the American colonies became independent, and the tobacco trade stopped. Heavy industry began to develop. It used coal and iron from the Clyde valley. Glasgow became rich but very dirty.

George Square ▼   *Glasgow University* ▶

Rangers and Celtic

Glasgow has two famous football teams: Glasgow Rangers and Celtic. Most people in Glasgow are fans of one of these teams. When they play against each other, thousands of fans go to watch.

Rangers and Celtic have won more football competitions in Scotland than all the other Scottish teams. In 1967 Celtic won the most important football competition in Europe, the European Cup. In 1972 Rangers won another European competition, the Cupwinners' Cup.

The Falls of Clyde and New Lanark

25 miles (40 km) above Glasgow the River Clyde enters a narrow valley. You can walk along the side of the valley and look down at the river 50 metres below you. You will see three great waterfalls, one of them 20 metres high. These are the Falls of Clyde.

In 1785 two Scots built a cotton factory at the bottom of the valley. By 1799 it was the biggest factory in Scotland and 2,000 workers lived in the village. The name of the village was New Lanark. The factory closed in 1968 but many tourists visit the village and its factory because Robert Owen worked there in the early days of the factory.

Robert Owen is famous because he tried to help the workers in his factory. He built an institute for adults. They could read and talk there. In those days young children often worked in

factories. Robert Owen did not like that. At New Lanark, no children under ten worked in the factories. Young children went to a nursery and older children went to a school.

The Ayrshire Coast

From Glasgow we go down the River Clyde and then turn
south along the coast of the Firth of Clyde. The views across
the sea are very beautiful. First we can see the mountains of
the Island of Arran. Then we see the great rock of Ailsa Craig.
It stands 335 metres out of the water. Finally we see the coast
of Ireland.

On the way we pass many famous golf courses like Troon,
Prestwick and Turnberry. We also pass old castles. The most
beautiful is Culzean Castle. Here we can see the famous round
sitting room and walk in the gardens.

It is important to stop at the Electric Brae, a few miles south
of Ayr. We can stop our car and take off the brake. Then we
will start to move slowly uphill!

Robert Burns (1759–1796)

One of the most famous houses in Scotland is at Alloway, near Ayr. It is very small but thousands of people visit it each year. Robert Burns was born in this house in 1759.

Burns was a farmer but he was always poor. He became famous because he wrote poetry. He wrote many love poems and some of these are now songs. Perhaps you know

My love is like a red, red rose.

Burns also wrote angry poems about rich people and poor people. For Burns all men were the same. They were all brothers. He wrote

The honest man, though e'er sae poor
Is King o' men, for a' that.

e'er sae = ever so
o' = of
a' = all
= A man can be very poor, but he is still important.

45

Tam o'Shanter

Burns was born on 25 January. Scots people have a party in the evening of that day. They eat haggis, a large sausage, and listen to a talk about Burns and to his poetry. A popular poem is *Tam o'Shanter*.

Tam went to a pub in Ayr and stayed there till midnight. On his way home he passed the church at Alloway. He saw lights in the church and looked inside. He saw witches and devils, and they saw him. They came out of the church and tried to catch him. On the bridge over the river Doon, one witch caught his horse's tail. But Tam and his horse were safe because the witches could not cross water.

Auld Lang Syne

Rich people in Edinburgh liked Burns's love poems but they did not like his other poems. They did not help him much. They gave him a small job in Dumfries. So Burns left his farm and went to Dumfries. There he died in 1796.

AULD LANG SYNE

1. Should auld acquaintance be forgot,
    And never bro't to mind?
    Should auld acquaintance be forgot,
    And days of auld lang syne?
Chorus: For auld lang syne, my dear,
    For auld lang syne,
    We'll tak' a cup o' kindness yet
    For auld lang syne.

From Dumfries it is only 30 miles (64 km) to England and we must say goodbye to Scotland. But first we must sing Burns's most famous poem.

auld = old
forgot = forgotten
acquaintance = You and I were friends long ago = in the days of our *aquaintance*
auld lang syne = the days of long ago
brought to min' (mind) = remembered
We do not want to forget the days of our aquaintance and never to remember them. We do not want to forget the days of our aquaintance and the days of long ago. So, my friend, we will have a drink and remember the days of long ago.

Addison Wesley Longman Limited,
Edinburgh Gate, Harlow,
Essex CM20 2JE, England
and Associated Companies throughout the world.

First published 1986
Ninth impression 1996

ISBN 0-582-53346-5

Set in Linotron 202 Plantin
Printed in China
EPC/09

Acknowledgements
We should like to thank the following for permission to reproduce the photographs: All-Sport Limited for page 42 (David Cannon); Aspect Picture Library Limited for page 30 (bottom); Barnabys Picture Library for pages 31 and 43; BBC Hulton Picture Library for pages 10, 12 (top), 13, 19, 27 (left), 35, 45 (left) and 46; British Petroleum Company p.l.c for page 25 (top), and for supplying the map reference on page 25 (bottom); British Tourist Authority for page 41; Camera Press Limited for page 26 (Patrick Lichfield); J. Allan Cash Limited for page 7 (bottom right); Donald Cooper for page 20 (left) (photos from the 1983 RSC production); Daily Telegraph Colour Library for page 24 (bottom) (John Sims); Dominic Photography for page 8; Susan Griggs Agency Limited for page 22 (Adam Woolfitt); The Image Bank for pages 27 (right) (Charles Weckler) and 36 (D'Lynn Waldron); Longman Photo Unit for page 39 (top); The Mansell Collection for pages 12 (bottom) and 15; Mary Evans Picture Library for pages 7 (top), 11 (right) and 34; The National Portrait Gallery for page 33; The Photographers Library for page 14 (top); The Photo Source Limited for pages 21 (top), 32, 40 and 44; Pictor International Limited for page 29; Picturepoint Limited for page 30 (top); Singer Sewing Machine Company for page 39 (middle and bottom); Scottish Tourist Board for page 7 (bottom left); Sporting Pictures (UK) Limited for page 21 (bottom); Tony Stone Photo Library/London for pages 6, 14 (bottom), 18 (bottom), 23, 24 (top), 28, 38 and 45 (right); Topham Picture Library for page 11 (left); Andy Williams Photographic Library for pages 9, 18 (top), and 37; Woodmansterne for pages 16-17 (Jeremy Marks).

Cover photograph by The Photographers Library.

Illustrations by Clifford Meadway